360°

Success Magnet

Heri Marco

360°

Success Magentic

Heri Marco

Published in the United Republic of Tanzania by
Research & Development Network.
The website address is www.rdnplatform.org

DEDICATION

This book is dedicated to my sons, Hefan and Hefard. You are born to reign. Be fruitful, multiply, fill the earth, and subdue it with justice and righteousness. The opportunities are around you in 360 degrees. Go, my friends; attract it. Discover the uncharted opportunities, and let your visions carry you to places you're predestined. For in the boundless expanse of possibility lies a life of all opportunities as far as your eyes can see.

CONTENTS

ACKNOWLEDGMENTS

I acknowledge the grace of the Lord Jesus Christ, God's love, and the Holy Spirit's fellowship in writing this book. I believe all good things about life and Godliness come from God. The power to create wealth and wisdom comes from God. I am so thankful to God for all the facts and fresh wisdom presented in this book to inspire us to create intergenerational wealth.

I appreciate the contribution of my wife, Edditrice Marco. Thank you for being a faithful partner in learning about our nature and life. You have been my best friend and partner since I started the journey of discovering our true identity. You stood by me in every season. That is true friendship.

To my sons, Hefan and Hefard. Thank you for being good students and leaders. My great joy is to hear that you are walking in the truth.

Chapter

1

Opportunities

Potential opportunities are always around us in 360 degrees. We live with opportunities every day. We meet with opportunities everywhere we go. One of the strategic challenges facing many people is how to discover and explore these opportunities. It has been harder to discover opportunities than challenges and probes. When you conduct a public interview about life experience, many people will spot the obstacles and problems they face. You can rarely find people who spot opportunities in those challenges and difficulties.

When you ask people about starting a business or investment opportunities, most need help with what to do. They do not see any potential opportunities around them. It is complex; there are many questions to answer.

How can I see it?
How can I manage it?
Is it possible?
What if I lost my fund?

About 99 percent of people need help to spot and unlock potential opportunities in 360 degrees. It is easier to spot challenges or problems than opportunities.

Less than 1% can discover and unlock potential opportunities in 360 degrees. These are people who see challenges and problems as opportunities. They think and develop solutions to our society's challenges and problems and generate a lot of money. Many successful people have used potential opportunities in 360 degrees to create Multiple Sources of Income to ensure the sustainability of their financial wealth.

This book presented potential opportunities in 360 degrees that anybody can discover and explore. These are potential business and investment opportunities within and beyond talent. If you are talented in music, you can be a successful musician. Also, you have a great chance to succeed in any business or investment in the music sector. For example, you can invest in a music studio, mentor, or join a music academy. These are an opportunity within talent.

Beyond talent are business or investment opportunities that you can explore beyond the area you're good at. The easiest way to explore these opportunities is to attract via success magnetic created by your market value. The 360 degrees of potential opportunities around you include opportunities within and beyond talent.

Potential opportunities 360 degrees

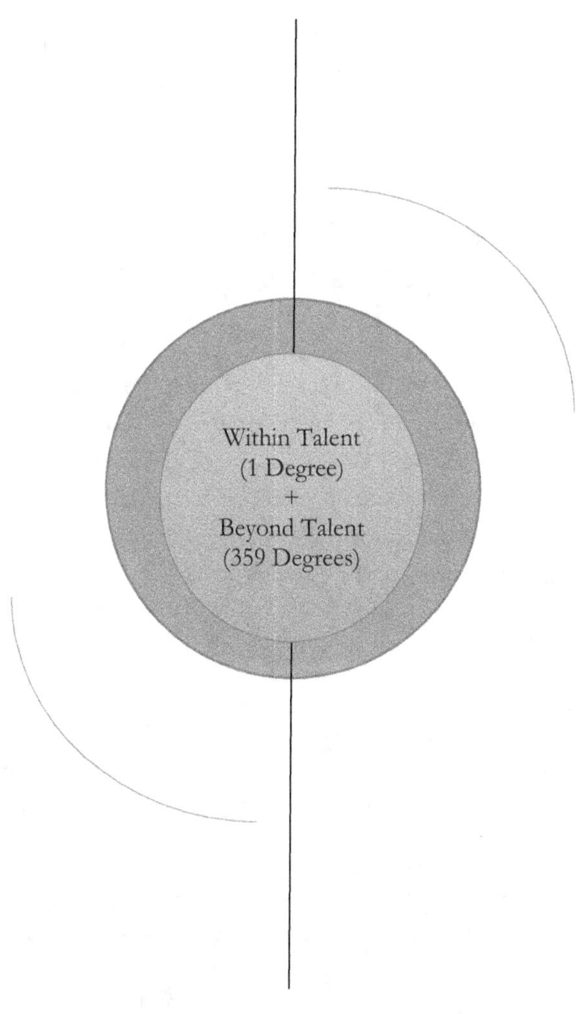

WITHIN TALENT

The opportunities within talent count one degree of potential opportunities around you. Discovering opportunities within your talent is easy because they link directly with what you love and do the best. Working within your talent is the best since you work at the highest level of your natural ability. It is working at what you are good at and with high ability.

Working within your talent counts only one degree of potential opportunities around you. It is the first area anybody can invest in to create multiple sources of income to ensure the sustainability of their financial wealth.

Though there are many successful people, most have yet to maximize even the opportunities within their talents (1 degree). If the current successful people, who comprise 1% of the world population, decide to maximize the investment within their abilities, their financial wealth would be more than they have today. The following are examples of potential opportunities within your talent.

Sports

You're good at football. You have a great opportunity to be a professional paid footballer, or open football academy, or be football coach, or invest in production of football equipment, and other opportunities linked to football.

You're good at baseball. You have a great opportunity to be professional paid basketball player, or open basketball academy, or invest in manufacturing basketball equipment and other opportunities linked with basketball.

You're good at athletics. You have a great opportunity to be a successful Athleticism, or be athletics coach or open athletics academy.

You're good at boxing. You have a great opportunity to be professional boxer, or be boxing coacher, or open boxing academy, or fitness center, or invest in manufacturing boxing equipment and other opportunities in boxing sport.

You're good at tenisball. You have a great opportunity to be professional tenisball player, or be a coacher, or open tenisball training center, or invest in manufacturing tenisball equipment and other opportunities in tenisball sport.

You're good at golf. You have a great opportunity to be professional golf player, or be a coacher, or open golf training center, or invest in manufacturing of golf equipment and other opportunities in golf sport.

Art Industry

You're good at music. You have an excellent opportunity to be a professional musician, open a music studio or academy, be a music mentor or coach, and have other opportunities in music.

You're good at dancing. You have an excellent opportunity to be a professional dancer, open a dancing studio or academy, be a dancer mentor, coach, and other opportunities in the dancing area.

You're good at painting or sculpture, carpentry, and designing. You have a great opportunity to open a painting, sculpture, and furniture store. You have an excellent chance to open a painting, sculpture, and carpentry training center.

You're good at baking. You have an excellent opportunity to be a professional baker, open barkery, a barkery training center, or supply bakery equipment and other opportunities in the baking area.

You're good at cooking. You can be a professional cooker or open a catering service and cooking training center.

You're good at creativity and design. You have an excellent opportunity to be a designer and fashion designer, opening creative and designing training centers, designing television shows, and supplying design works.

You're good at gardening. You have an excellent opportunity to be a professional Gardner in open garden centers, gardening homes and offices, and open garden training centers.

You're good at comedy and joking. You have an excellent opportunity to be a professional comedian, open comedy shows on TV or YouTube, and open a comedy training center.

You're good at acting. You have an excellent opportunity to be a professional actor, a movie director, or open an acting training center and movie production firm.

You're good at singing. You can be a professional singer or open a singing academy and music production firm.

You're guitar playing. You can be a professional guitar player or open a music studio or guitar training academy.

Health

You're a talented and successful healthcare worker; you address health issues. You have an excellent opportunity to open a hospital, clinic, laboratory, dispensary, or an online platform for health issues or open a pharmacy and other opportunities in the health area. Ben Carson and many successful health leaders succeeded in using their inborn ability to make a difference and build their success magnet.

Information Technology

You're good at computer literacy, or computers. You have an excellent opportunity to train people in computer skills, open a computer shop and a computer workshop.

You're good at software and digital technology. You have an excellent opportunity to establish an online marketing service, develop IT systems and applications, design and production services, and other opportunities linked with Information Technology. Jeff Bezos, Bill Gates, and many successful leaders succeeded in using their inborn ability to make a difference and build their success magnet.

Science and Technology

You're good at science and technology. You have an excellent opportunity to innovate and invent different services and products. Sir Isaac Newton succeeded in discovering Newton's Law by using his inborn ability in science to make a difference in science. Steve Jobs succeeded in creating the first computer by using his inborn ability to make a difference in technology. Elon Musk succeeded in inventing the electric vehicle known as Tesla by using its inborn ability to create a difference in the motor industry. Einstein Albert succeeded in discovering many scientific investors by using their inborn ability to make a difference. In general, successful people use their inborn ability to create a difference and become magnets of success.

Leadership

You're good at leadership. You can be a political leader, religious leader, arm leader, business leader, or Chief Executive Officer. You're good at decision-making. You have an excellent opportunity to be a professional leader, establish leadership coaching and mentorship, or establish a leadership academy and other opportunities in leadership. John Maxwell and many successful leaders succeeded in using their inborn ability to make a difference and built a success magnet.

Motivation & Inspiration

You're good at motivating, inspiring, encouraging enthusiasm, positivism, initiative, and persuasiveness. You have the opportunity to be a professional motivational speaker, be a mentor and other opportunities in motivation. Tony Robbin, Jack Canfield, Less Brown, and many successful leaders succeeded in using their inborn ability to make a difference.

You access these opportunities within your talent and create Multiple Sources of Income (MSIs). These opportunities count as one (1) degree of the potential opportunities around you. The following diagram illustrates opportunities within talent. The area presents the opportunities within talent shaded red. It counts only 1 degree of potential opportunities around you.

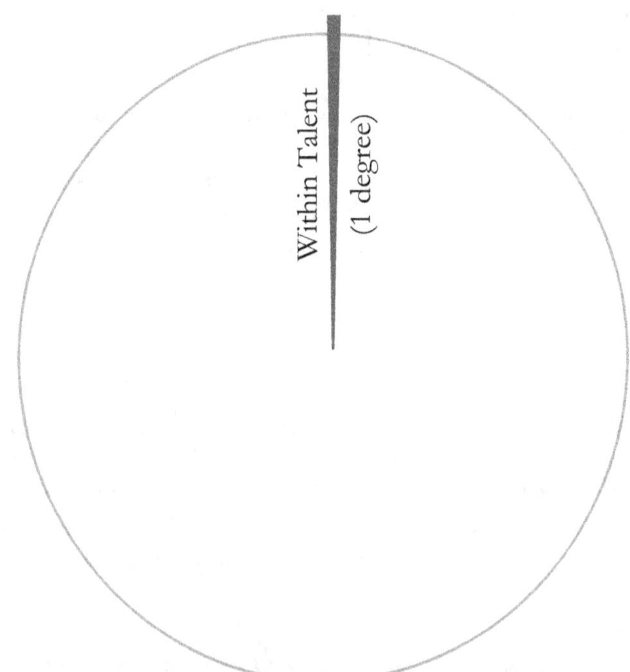

BEYOND TALENT

Beyond talent are potential business and investment opportunities beyond the area that you're good at. It counts 359 out of 360 degrees of all possible opportunities around your life. About 99.7 percent of opportunities around you are beyond talent. The opportunities within talent count for only 0.3 percent of all opportunities around you. Many successful people succeeded in investing in opportunities within their talent. There are few successful people and mostly the wealthiest families in the world who go beyond talent to explore opportunities in 360 degrees. The grey color area represents opportunities beyond talent. It counts 359 degrees of potential opportunities around you.

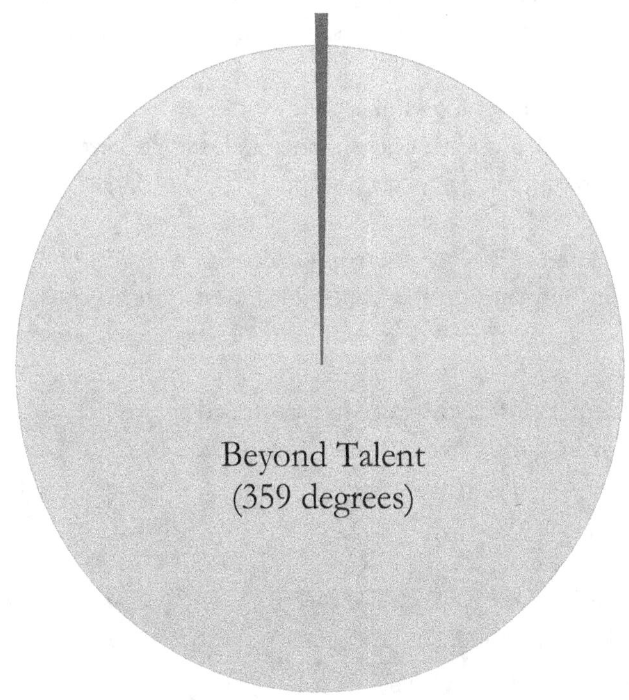

Talented and successful people can invest beyond talent to access potential business and investment opportunities in 359 degrees. Talented and successful people can access business and investment opportunities at the global, continental, regional block, country, region, district, ward, village, school, street, and family levels. Anybody can access opportunities beyond talent, which counts 359 degrees of potential opportunities around us;

> A talented and successful musician can invest in opportunities within and out of the music industry to access potential opportunities in 360 degrees.

> A talented and successful Public Speaker can invest in opportunities within and outside the public speaking industry to access potential opportunities in 360 degrees.

> A talented and successful economist can invest in opportunities within and outside the economics industry to access potential opportunities in 360 degrees.

> A talented and successful basketball can invest in opportunities within and outside the basketball industry to access potential opportunities in 360 degrees.

> A talented and successful Motivation and Inspiration coach can invest in opportunities within and outside the motivation and inspiration industry to access potential opportunities in 360 degrees.

> A talented and successful leader from any sector can invest in the leadership industry and other industries to access potential opportunities in 360 degrees.

A talented and successful comedian can invest in the comedian business and other industries to access potential opportunities in 360 degrees.

A talented and successful Artist can invest in the Art industry and other industries to access potential opportunities in 360 degrees.

Many success philosophers will advise focusing on opportunities within talent and passion. It is the best advice if you do it yourself. But intelligent people who use the money to work for them go beyond talent to explore opportunities in 360 degrees. Focusing on your core genius is suitable for building your success magnet. When the success magnet is powerful, you no longer need to concentrate on opportunities within talent. You go for 360 degrees of potential opportunities to create integration wealth.

Chapter

2

Magnet

A magnet is a material or object that produces a magnetic field. This magnetic field is invisible but is responsible for the most notable property of a magnet: a force that attracts or pulls on other ferromagnetic materials, such as iron, steel, nickel, and cobalt, and attracts or repels other magnets.

The easiest way to attract ferromagnetic materials such as iron, nickel, cobalt, and others is by using a magnet.

It is easy to attract all iron in the field using a magnet.

It is easy to attract steel in the field using a magnet.

It is easy to attract nickel in the field using a magnet.

Your high productivity in collecting iron or nickel depends on the power of the magnet and on how you use the magnet. The power of a magnet depends on the capital invested in developing the magnet.

There is an inborn success architect in you. This successful architect is a magnet to all success in life. Success can be in business, a career, and life in general. Talent and passion are success architects or magnets within you, attracting success if well nurtured. Everyone has these inborn success architects, for we are God's handiwork, created in Christ Jesus to do good works, which God prepared us to do (Ephesians 2:10).

A well-nurtured and used talent and passion produce a magnetic field or success magnet that attracts success in life. The success magnet is the invisible force that attracts success in life. Your success magnet is equivalent to your market value.

It depends on how much you invested in nurturing and using your talent, passion, and skills. The higher the investment in nurturing and using your talent, love, and skills needed, the higher the success magnet and vice versa is true.

The success magnet gives you a brand. You become the brand according to the success magnet or market value. You attract all potential opportunities in 360 degrees according to the market value or magnetic field.

Talented and successful people like Warren Buffet, Leones Mess, Christian Ronaldo, David Beckham, Jeff Bezos, and others are successful because they nurtured their success magnet. Their market values unlock all possible opportunities in 360 degrees. They are welcome to invest in any industry and country. Their limit to invest in potential opportunities in 360 degrees is their fear.

Highly nurtured and using talent, passion, and skill, develop a powerful success magnet or market value that attracts all possible opportunities in 360 degrees. You command the investment according to your market value or success magnet.

The easiest way to attract success is to invest in developing and using talent and doing what you love. It is natural to work like that.

Your high productivity in building success in life depends on the power of your success magnet. The more you invest in nurturing and using the talent, passion, and skills needed to achieve the best, the more you develop a powerful success magnet, and vice versa is true. The success magnet attracts all possibilities and opportunities according to the level of investment. It is a door to all possibilities and opportunities in 360 degrees.

Discovering, nurturing, and using your talent and passion is necessary to access opportunities in 360 degrees. Everyone is created for a purpose and well equipped with all the success architects need to live a fulfilled life. You must understand your talent and passion. Your inner man in your heart understands more about your talent. If you are not working in the area where you are good at, you might experience some complaints. Why should you try or work in that job or business? Most of the time, we are not open to listening to our hearts. We listen mostly to our minds and keep doing things without considering whether we are good at it. You limit yourself to achieving the best in life by not using your talent. Take time and work on yourself, assess what you are good at, and invest to develop and use.

You can do the best for any business or job if you decide. But you can never be extraordinary in any business or career. You can only be exceptional in business or a job with natural ability. Remember, we are God's handiwork, created in Christ Jesus to do good works, which God prepared us to do.

There are many talents in the world endowed in every human being. The following are examples of talents from different industries. Discover your talent and persuade it. You can be good at dealing with failure, focus, handle change, make friends, spot new trends, academics, accounting, adaptability, advertising, affiliate systems, analyzing the past, art, articulate, asking questions, athleticism, awareness, bookkeeping, brainstorming, communication skills, computer literacy, computers, conflict resolution, creativity, critical thinking, decision making, detail orientation, dexterity, drawing, empathy, encouraging, enthusiasm, fairness, financial management, financial planning, foreign language, future thinking, futuristic, graphics, guerrilla marketing, health, fitness, high energy, hiring, recruiting, human resources, identify strengths and weaknesses, imagination, imaginative, initiative, innovation, inspiring, integrity, honesty, intuition, inventiveness, jokes or humor, juggling, leadership, learner, legal, listening, logistics, magic, maintenance or routine tasks, making connections, marketing, math, meeting management, money management, music, negotiating skills, photography, planning, problem solving, public speaking, raise money, reading, relaxation, relieve stress, research, risk management, sales, singing, storytelling, taxes, teaching, writing and many other areas a few to mention.

A highly nurtured and used talent and passion produce a magnet that can easily link you to all possible opportunities around you. Using your talent, you can be productive and attract more opportunities.

Discover what you are capable of doing. Nurture and use it optimally.
Discover what you love to do. Nurture and use it optimally.
Discover what skills are needed. Nurture and use it optimally.

Go deeper in your spirit, meditate, and ask your higher self. Ask your parents, teachers, and mentors. They will advise you. Invest in nurturing and using talent, passion, and skill to develop success magnets in your life.

Chapter

3

Magnetic Field

A magnet field is the invisible power of a magnet that attracts other ferromagnetic materials. The power of the magnetic field depends on the capital invested in developing the magnet. The higher the investment, the higher the power of the magnetic field, and vice versa, is true.

The magnet field works the same way the success magnet works. The success magnet is the invisible force that attracts success in life. Remember, a success magnet is a product of nurturing and using talent, passion, and skills needed. The way the magnet field attracts other ferromagnetic materials is the same way a success magnet attracts success according to what they believe is possible.

People who have succeeded in nurturing their talents, passions, and skills have developed a success magnet, which is equivalent to the market value. The market values give you a brand. You become the brand according to your market value. You attract all potential opportunities in 360 degrees according to the power of your success magnet. Talented and successful people have developed their success magnet and become a magnet to success. Their success magnet is a gateway to all potential opportunities in 360 degrees.

Highly nurtured and used talent, passion, and skill develop a powerful magnetic field or market value that can attract all potential opportunities in 360 degrees. You command the market according to your market value or magnetic field. The magnetic field or market value can attract success at different levels depending on the belief and the level of investment incurred in nurturing and using it.

Success magnet can command, influence, and attract all potential opportunities in 360 degrees at different levels. It all depends on the level of investment in nurturing and using talent, passion, and skills with a sound mindset. It also relies on what you believe in your mind. Higher investment produces a powerful success magnet, and vice versa is true. You attract success according to the power of your success magnet or how far your success magnet can reach.

Your success magnet can command, influence, and attract all potential at the family, street, village, ward, province, count, district, region, country, nation, continent, and global level. It all depends on the level of investment and what you believe is possible. Regardless of the level, utilizing all potential opportunities in 360 degrees is necessary.

GLOBAL

Some people believe it is possible to nurture their talents, passion, and skills needed to develop a magnetic field at the global level. They invest in nurturing and using their talents and passion to build a magnet of success worldwide. Talented and successful people who have developed success magnets at the global level can access potential opportunities around the world in 360 degrees.

Talented and successful people in sports like Leon Messi, Ronald, David Beckham, and others can access potential opportunities in 360 degrees from any country worldwide.

Talented and successful people in innovation and technology like Elon Musk, Bill Gates, Jeff Bezos, Jack Ma, and Mark Zuckerberg can access potential opportunities from any country worldwide in 360 degrees.

Talented and successful people in music like Beyonce, Rihana, 50 Cent, and Luck Dube can access potential opportunities from any country worldwide in 360 degrees.

They can meet with any successful business or political leaders worldwide. Their influence at the global level is the door to all opportunities around the world. They are welcome to invest in any industry and country. Their limit to invest in possible opportunities in 360 degrees is their fear. It is the same for all talented and successful people in any industry.

CONTINENT

Some people believe it is possible to nurture their talent, passion, and skills needed to develop a success magnet at the continent level. They invest in nurturing and using their abilities, love, and skills required to create their magnetic field at the continent level.

Talented and successful people who have developed magnetic fields at the continent level can access potential opportunities at the continent level in 360 degrees. Some gifted and successful people have developed success magnets in a specific continent. It can be Africa, Asia, Europe, South America, North America or Australia.

Talented and successful people who have developed the success magnet at the continent level can access potential opportunities within the continent in 360 degrees. Their success magnet at the continent level is the door to all opportunities within the continent. They can access all potential opportunities at a continent level in 360 degrees.

COUNTRY

Some people believe it is possible to nurture their talent, passion, and skills needed to develop success magnet at country level. They invest in nurturing and using their talents, passion, and skills to build their success magnet at the country level. For example, there are talented and successful people who developed success magnets within the United States of America, the United Kingdom, China, Russia, France, Tanzania, Australia, Brazil, Nigeria, Kenya, Morocco, South Africa, Rwanda, Ethiopia, United Emirates Arabs, Qatar, Argentina and other countries.

Talented and successful people who have developed their success magnet at the country level can access all potential opportunities within the country in 360 degrees. Their success magnet at the country level is a door to all possible opportunities within the country in 360 degrees. They can access all potential opportunities at the country level in 360 degrees.

STATE OR REGION

Some people believe it is possible to nurture their talent, passion, and skills needed to develop a success magnet at the state or regional level. They invest in nurturing and using their talents, passion, and skills to build their success magnet at the state or regional level. For example, talented and successful people developed success magnets in New York States, London, Paris, Tokyo, Washington, Abuja, Nairobi, Dar es Salaam, Cape Town, Guanzhou, Kigali, and others.

Talented and successful people who have developed their success magnet at the state or regional level can access all potential opportunities in 360 degrees. Their success magnet at the state or regional level is the door to all possible opportunities in 360 degrees. They can access all potential state or region-level opportunities in 360 degrees.

DISTRICT

Some people believe it is possible to nurture their talent, passion, and skills needed to develop a district-level success magnet. They invest in nurturing and using their talents, passion, and skills to build their success magnet field at the district level.

Talented and successful people who have developed success magnets at the district level can access all possible potential opportunities in 360 degrees. Their success magnet at the district level is the door to all possible opportunities in 360 degrees. They can access all potential opportunities at the district level in 360 degrees.

TOWN OR CITY

Some people believe it is possible to nurture their talent, passion, and skills to develop a success magnet at the town or city level. They invest in nurturing and using their talents, passion, and skills to create a success magnet at the town or city level.

Talented and successful people who have developed success magnets at the town or city level can access all potential opportunities in 360 degrees. Their success magnet at the town or city level is the door to all possible opportunities in 360 degrees. They can access all potential opportunities at the town or city level in 360 degrees.

WARD OR VILLAGE

Some people believe it is possible to nurture their talent, passion, and skills to develop a success magnet in a specific ward or village. They invest in nurturing and using their talents, passion, and skills to create a success magnet in a particular ward or village.

Talented and successful people who have developed success magnets in a specific ward or village can access all potential opportunities in 360 degrees. Their success magnet at the ward or town is the door to all possible opportunities in 360 degrees. They can access all potential opportunities within the ward or village in 360 degrees.

STREET

Some people believe it is possible to nurture their talents, passions, and skills needed to develop a street-level success magnet. They invest in nurturing and using their talents, passion, and skills required to create success magnets at the street level.

Talented and successful people who have developed success magnets at the street level can access all possible potential opportunities in 360 degrees. Their street-level success magnet is the door to all possible opportunities in 360 degrees. They can access all potential opportunities at street level in 360 degrees.

FAMILY

Some people believe it is possible to nurture their talent, passion, and skills needed to develop success magnet at family level. They invest in nurturing and using their talents, passion, and skills to create a success magnet at the family level.

Talented and successful people who have developed success magnets at the family level can access all potential opportunities in 360 degrees. Their family-level success magnet is the door to all possible opportunities in 360 degrees. They can access all potential opportunities within the family in 360 degrees.

Chapter

4

Season

There are seasons for everything in life. The magnetic field of your talent has seasons. Potential business and investment opportunities have seasons. But there is no perfect time to nurture and use the talent, passion, and skills you need for success in life. This book presents three seasons for the magnetic field of your talent. These seasons include growth, pick, and decline. Each season determines the power of your success magnet or market value.

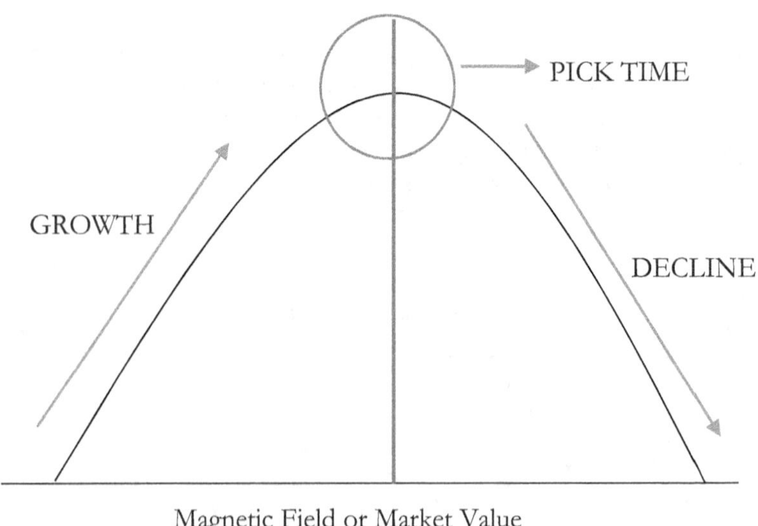

GROWTH SEASON

The growth season is when you are improving in building your success magnet by nurturing and using your talent, passion, and skills. During this season, you invest and cultivate your body, mind, and spirit to succeed in what you love and do the best. Growth season comes when you undergo training and coaching in business, school, college, university, and life. It is the season when your productivity is at the growth stage. You are working hard to influence everything to work in your favor and develop a success magnet. It is the time when:-

> You depart from your comfort zone to invest and nurture your talent, passion, skills, and belief.

> You keep investing more in nurturing talent and becoming known to the market.

> You work hard and get paid less. Remember, you get paid high at the pick-up time.

> You start commanding influence at different levels: world, continent, nation, state, region, district, village, street, or family.

> You begin to achieve the best by using your talent in doing what you love.

Growth season is a good season for your body, mind, and spirit growth. You may not be more attractive to potential opportunities in 360 degrees because you're still developing your market value. The main focus in this season is to keep investing and nurturing your talent, passion, and skill needed for success to reach the picking season. Nobody invests for nothing. You require a return on investment. Therefore, reaching the picking season is the goal for anyone who desires to achieve the best in life. You have to invest in your talent to create your market value. The growth strategy for anyone who wants to reach the pick and be successful is to invest and nurture talent.

PICK SEASON

The picking season is when the investment in nurturing your talent, passion, and skills needed to succeed in life produces the highest magnetic field or success magnet. The picking season is when you perform at the pick in your business, job, and other life investments. It is the season when your productivity is at its highest. It is the time when you achieve the best. It is the time when you're very famous for doing what you love by using talent. It can be sports, art, writing, public speaking, business, technology, innovation, research, and others. You're at the highest level of approval and acceptance in the industry and the community. You become the brand of who you are regarding the talent, passion, skills, and beliefs you have developed.

It is when people worldwide and from different continents, nations, states, regions, districts, villages, and streets are looking at you.

It is when the world's business, political, and religious leaders are looking at you.

It is when everything works in your favor. You're in high demand in the market. It might be:-

> You're performing well. You received the award as the best professional footballer in the World, continent, Country, Regional or province, district, count, ward, village, street, or family.

> You're doing well. You received the award as the best writer in the World, continent, country, region, province, and district count.

> You're challenging the status quo. You received an award as the best IT professional in the World, continent, Country, Regional or province, district, count, ward, village, street, or family.

> You're outperforming in the market. You received the award as the best musician in the World, continent, Country, Regional or

province, district, count, ward, village, street, or family.

You're doing well in the market. You received an award as the best public speaker in the World, continent, Country, Regional or province, district, count, ward, village, street, or family.

You're the best basketball player in the World, continent, Country, Regional or province, district, count, ward, village, street, or family.

You're the best boxer in the World, continent, Country, Regional or province, district, count, ward, village, street, or family.

You're the best carate player in the World, continent, country, region, or province.

You're Miss World, Continent, Country, Regional or province, district, count, ward, village, street, or family.

Pick season is limited in terms of time. It lasts so fast. You must smart enough to maintain it. Remember, during your pick season, you will keep growing in age, and new champions will arise every day. So, you have a short time to discover and explore potential opportunities in 360 degrees.

Many talented and successful people maintain at pick season for a short time and others for a long time. It depends on your strategy and how you balance the pull and push factors. The picking season differs from one industry to another and from one person to another. It depends on how you have prepared to maintain those push and pull factors.

Pick season is the best for anyone who desires to invest in potential opportunities and create Multiple Sources of Income. Some talented and successful people are satisfied with the wealth created during the picking season and lose it in less than ten years. Regardless of what amount of money they are paying or what you're making now, you need more than one source of income to ensure your financial sustainability. You need to invest and diversify your financial wealth by creating a sound multiple source of income in 360 degrees. Capitalize on pick season to tape potential opportunities in 360 degrees. You have every chance to meet any leaders, either political leaders or business leaders, during pick season. You have an excellent opportunity to meet successful people. You can meet, connect, and discuss with any CEO from any organization or bank and many business and investment opportunities.

The picking season is the most valuable time in your life. Either you use it very effectively, or you regret it in the future. When you ask many football players, musicians, politicians, artists, and others who did not capitalize in pick season, they regret it. Why I didn't do this during that time? I got many opportunities, but why? And so many questions. Pick season usually comes once; it may repeat if you're so lucky. It is essential to understand your pick season and use it strategically to explore potential opportunities and create multiple sources of income.

The journey to the picking season might be easier than maintaining momentum in the picking season. The picking season needs high discipline to maintain push and pull factors. Self-discipline is required to control your behavior and character. It needs self-discipline in time management, financial planning, talent development, self-practices, and adherence to the best practices.

Pick season needs close attention from your teacher and mentor. Your teacher and mentor have a great chance to help you maintain for a long time during your pick season. If you have a good teacher and mentor with experience, they can assist you if you listen. It is the time that you need more practice and learning than ever. More training and education will help you to improve and maintain.

Stay calm with your famous during pick season. Turn those praise and fame into energy to attract and invest in potential opportunities. You need smart people around you who can advise you on great business and investment opportunities to create multiple sources of income. The pick time is the most profitable and dangerous; you need to think more wisely and use it strategically to explore potential business and investment opportunities in 360 degrees. It will help you create multiple sources of income to ensure financial sustainability from decades to decades.

DECLINE SEASON

Pick season is the most challenging time to maintain the momentum. That's why there is a decline season where your magnetic field or success magnet begins to decline. The world starts to shift attention from you towards new emerging talents. Many factors make people decline from the picking season. These factors include the emergence of new people with high talent value. Emerging new talents with high market value may push you out of pick season if you lack the commitment and discipline to maintain the momentum.

Generally, decline season means:-
You have achieved the best, but you have decided to retire.
You have achieved the best but have yet to maintain the momentum.

The decline season is better than the growth season regarding attracting potential opportunities in 360 degrees. You still have a high brand and command to attract potential business and investment opportunities in 360 degrees. You can still maximize the investments in 360 degrees if you missed it during the picking season. But it depends on the industry and your talent. For example, talented and successful people in sports and other sectors may maximize investment in 360 degrees during the declining season because pick season is busy. After retiring at age 34, David Beckham used his savings to invest in a horse ranch, a football academy, and fashion.

Decline season is the last resort for anyone wanting to attract potential investment in 360 degrees.

Decline season is the season of diversifying what you have accumulated during the picking season to create multiple sources of income.

Chapter

5

System

Creating and transferring financial wealth for many generations is a goal for everyone. But it has not been accessible to many people. Two thousand years ago, many believed that wealth would never survive three generations. This belief or proverb is translated as "Fu bu quo san dai" in China Proverb, "clogs to clogs in three generations" in Europe, and "shirtsleeves to shirtsleeves" in the United States. This statement implies that when the first generation gains family wealth, the second generation maintains the family fortune, and the third generation loses it.

Regardless of the three-generation pattern, there are talented and successful families who have succeeded in maintaining their wealth for more than three generations. The Rothschilds, Rockefellers, and Walton families proved that attracting wealth and keeping it for many generations is possible. These families created wealth by nurturing their talents, passions, skills, and beliefs. Remember, a good man leaves an inheritance to his children's children, and the sinner's wealth is laid up for the just.

This book provides a simple model for people who have succeeded in developing a success magnet to invest in potential opportunities in 360 degrees and create generational wealth. This book does not guarantee or provide any legal advice that you will be successful by using these simple models. Use this model, learn more, and listen to your investment or financial advisor before investing your money. This book provides simple guides on the best business and investment model to create multiple income sources. This book echoes the same model used by successful families to maintain their financial wealth for many generations. Everybody has a chance to develop various sources of income to ensure the sustainability of economic wealth for many generations.

There are different models that you can invest in to create multiple sources of income and ensure the sustainability of your financial wealth for many generations. Many wealthy families who succeeded in maintaining their financial wealth from generation to generation have used these models. These models include ownership, lending, and cash investment. Regardless of the risks associated with the investment model, you must invest. That is the only way to create integration wealth. Remember that the most significant risk in life is to risk nothing. All successful people who succeeded in creating integration wealth took calculated risks. Even today, their families take calculated risks to keep their wealth from generation to generation.

OWNERSHIP

Ownership investments are investments that involve purchasing assets or businesses with the intent of acquiring an ownership stake. They generate a return on investment through asset value appreciation or dividend distribution.

Stocks

Investing in stocks can be a complex and nuanced process involving carefully considering the potential risks and rewards. Stocks represent ownership in a company as traded on stock exchanges worldwide. When you invest in stocks, you buy a small piece of a company and become a shareholder.

One of the key benefits of investing in stocks is the potential for high returns. Historically, stocks have provided higher returns than other asset classes, such as bonds or cash, over the long term. However, investing in stocks also involves a certain level of risk. Stocks are subject to market volatility and can experience significant price fluctuations in the short term.

It is essential to diversify your stock portfolio across different companies and industries. It can help reduce the impact of any company or industry experiencing significant losses. Additionally, investing in stocks is essential to have a long-term investment horizon. It will help if you prepare to hold onto your investments for several years or even decades, as stocks tend to produce higher returns over extended periods.

When investing in stocks, it's also important to consider your investment goals and risk tolerance. Some investors prefer to invest in blue-chip stocks, shares of large and well-established companies considered safer investments. Other investors may invest in growth stocks, which are shares of companies expected to grow faster than the overall market. These stocks can be more volatile in the short term but may offer higher potential returns over the long term.

Investing in stocks can be a great way to grow your wealth over the long term, but it's essential to understand the potential risks and rewards. By diversifying your portfolio, having a long-term investment horizon, and considering your investment goals and risk tolerance, you can maximize your returns while minimizing your risk. As with any investment, it's essential to research and seek advice from a financial professional before making any investment decisions.

Real Estate

Real estate investment involves the purchase, ownership, management, rental, or sale of real estate property to generate a profit. Real estate investments can take on many forms, such as residential or commercial properties, undeveloped land, or industrial buildings.

Investing in real estate can offer various benefits, including rental income, potential appreciation in value, tax benefits, and portfolio diversification. Real estate is also a tangible asset that investors can see and touch, providing a sense of security lacking in intangible investments like stocks and bonds.

However, investing in real estate can be complex and risky, as it requires significant financial resources, ongoing maintenance and management, and the potential for market fluctuations. Investors need to understand the real estate market and the specific property they are considering before investing. There are several ways to invest in real estate, such as direct ownership of properties, real estate investment trusts (REITs), real estate mutual funds, or crowdfunding platforms. Each investment method carries different requirements, risks, and potential returns.

Before investing in real estate, you should carefully consider your investment objectives, financial resources, risk tolerance, and market conditions. You should research and analyze the local real estate market, perform due diligence on potential properties, and seek professional advice before making investment decisions. It will be helpful if you prepare to actively manage the real estate investments, including dealing with tenants, repairs, maintenance, and keeping up with changing market conditions. These steps allow you to make informed decisions and maximize your returns from real estate investments.

Real Estate investment is one vehicle that has produced many millionaires in the United States of America. A statement says, if you want to be a millionaire, invest in real estate, but if you like to be a billionaire, invest in startup companies.

Business Ownership

Investments are made in startup companies with the expectation of significant returns if the company is successful. These investments can offer high returns. They carry varying risk levels, and assessing your investment objectives and risk tolerance is essential before investing. Careful research and analysis can help you decide which ownership investments fit your needs and goals. Investing in startups can be done through various channels, such as venture capital funds, angel investing, or crowdfunding platforms.

Venture capital funds are investment firms that provide capital to startups in exchange for an ownership stake in the company. These funds typically invest in startups that have already demonstrated a high growth potential and require a significant investment from the investor. The venture capital firm may also provide guidance and support to the startup to help ensure it reaches its potential. Venture capital investments can offer high returns if the startup is successful but also involve a high risk of failure. Investors need to perform due diligence on the venture capital firm and its investment portfolio to ensure they align with the investor's goals and objectives.

Angel investing involves individual investors providing capital to startups in exchange for an equity stake in the company. Angel investors typically invest smaller amounts of capital than venture capital firms and are often involved in the early stages of a startup's development. The investor may also guide and support the startup to help it grow and succeed. Angel investing can offer significant returns if the startup is booming but also involves a high risk of failure. Investors must perform due diligence on the startup and its management team to ensure they have the skills and experience necessary to succeed.

Crowdfunding platforms allow individual investors to pool their resources and invest in startups. As an investor, you receive an ownership stake in the company or through reward-based crowdfunding, where you receive non-equity rewards such as products or services. Crowdfunding investments can offer more accessible opportunities for small investors but also involve a high risk of failure. Investors need to research and analyze the crowdfunding platform and the startup before investing to ensure they align with the investor's goals and objectives.

Investing in startups requires careful consideration of the potential risks and rewards and a strong understanding of the industry and company in question. You must perform due diligence on potential investments, seek advice from financial and legal professionals, and diversify investments across different startups and industries. By taking these steps, you can maximize your returns from startup investments while mitigating the associated risks.

Business ownership investment is one of the vehicles that has made many billionaires in the United States of America. Many investors who invested in Amazon, Facebook, Airbnb, and other startups that currently are huge companies have received high returns on investment. Also, they will continue to gain in the lifetime of these companies. Since most startups end up listed on the stock market, they guarantee a return on investment from generation to generation. For example, people who invested in the New York Times have received dividends for over 172 years since 1851.

LENDING

Lending investment is an investment where an individual lends money to a borrower in exchange for interest payments over a certain period. The investment is made directly through peer-to-peer lending platforms or indirectly through investment funds specializing in lending.

One of the primary benefits of lending investment is the potential for a stable and predictable income stream, as the borrower is obligated to make regular interest payments on the loan. Depending on the loan terms and the borrower's creditworthiness, lending investments can offer higher returns than traditional fixed-income investments, such as bonds.

Lending investments also come with certain risks. It would help if you took a thorough analysis before investing. One of the main risks is the potential for the borrower to default on the loan, which could result in the loss of the invested capital. Lending investments depend on the changes in interest rates and economic conditions, which could affect the borrower's ability to make interest payments.

It is vital to conduct thorough due diligence on the borrower before making a lending investment. The due diligence may include reviewing the borrower's credit history, financial statements, and business plan. It's also important to diversify lending investments across different borrowers and industries to reduce the impact of any individual borrower defaulting on the loan.

When considering lending investments, it's also essential to understand the different types of available loans. Lending investment is secured when the borrower has pledged collateral to secure the loan. Collateral provides an additional layer of protection for the investor in the event of a default. Lending investment is unsecured when the borrower has not pledged any collateral. Unsecured loans can offer higher returns but can also be riskier.

Overall, lending investment can be a viable option for investors looking for a stable and predictable income stream. Still, it's necessary to carefully consider the potential risks and rewards before making any investment decisions. Seek the advice of a financial professional before making any investment decisions.

CASH

Cash investment is where an individual invests their money into low-risk securities, such as savings accounts, money market accounts, or certificates of deposit (CDs). It is the safest investment option as it typically offers a low return rate but carries minimal risk of loss.

One of the primary benefits of cash investment is the ease and accessibility of the investment options. Most banks and financial institutions offer various cash investment options that individuals can easily access. Savings accounts, for example, provide a simple way to earn interest on the money deposited in the account. The interest rate on savings accounts is typically lower than other investment options, such as stocks or bonds, but the account holder can withdraw the money at any time.

Another option is a money market account, which is similar to a savings account but typically offers a slightly higher interest rate. Money market accounts are also usually insured by the FDIC up to a certain amount, providing additional protection for investors.

Certificates of deposit (CDs) are another popular cash investment option. CDs offer a fixed interest rate for a set period, typically from a few months to several years. The interest rate on CDs is generally higher than savings or money market accounts, but the account holder must keep the money in the account for the term to earn the interest. Early withdrawal from a CD may result in penalties or fees.

However, cash investments also have certain drawbacks to consider before investing. One of the main drawbacks is the low rate of return, which may need to catch up with inflation. It means that over time, the purchasing power of the invested money may decrease. Additionally, some cash investment options may have penalties or fees for early withdrawal, impacting investors' ability to access their funds when needed.

To mitigate some of these risks, it's essential to carefully consider the different cash investment options available and choose an option that aligns with the investor's goals and risk tolerance. It's also important to regularly review and adjust the investment portfolio as needed to ensure it meets the investor's needs.

Cash investment can be a good option for investors looking for a low-risk investment option that offers ease and accessibility. However, it's essential to carefully consider the potential risks and rewards before making any investment decisions. Seek the advice of a financial professional before making any investment decisions.

ABOUT THE AUTHOR

Heri Marco is an entrepreneur, investor, author, and life coach. Heri loves to create solutions and empower others to be fruitful and have dominion over their lives. He is a founder of Research and Development Network.

Other books written by Heri Marco include Who Am I: Secret & Hidden Wisdom, The Art of Discovery & Innovation, Power of Success within You, 3X7X21 Success Formula, Social Media Success Supremacy and Success Architects.